IMAGES
of America

FORT MCALLISTER

IMAGES
of America

FORT MCALLISTER

Roger S. Durham

ARCADIA

Published by Arcadia Publishing
Charleston SC, Chicago IL, Portsmouth NH, San Francisco CA

Printed in Great Britain

Library of Congress Catalog Card Number: 2004106820

For all general information contact Arcadia Publishing at:
Telephone 843-853-2070
Fax 843-853-0044
E-mail sales@arcadiapublishing.com
For customer service and orders:
Toll-Free 1-888-313-2665

Visit us on the internet at http://www.arcadiapublishing.com

Dedicated to my girls at home who put up with me—JoAnn, Star, and Lacy

CONTENTS

Acknowledgments   6

Introduction   7

1.   The Battery and Genesis Point   9

2.   Iron and Sand   17

3.   The *Nashville*   37

4.   Sherman Comes   51

5.   The Final Assault   59

6.   The 20th Century   79

7.   Fort McAllister—Then and Now   97

ACKNOWLEDGMENTS

Individuals

Dr. Lawrence Babits
Charles Baisden
William Barnes
Paul Blatner
Mary H. (Nell) Bonaud
Caroline Bosbyshell
Phil Brinson
Danny Brown
Sam Brown
Keith Carter
Frank Chance
Paul Chance
Phil Coleman
Jim Cooler
Eulie Cowart
Ralph Cox
Tom Dale
Spanky Dent

Tom Dickey
Dr. John Duncan
Johnny Eason
Bill Fanning
Jay Graybeal
Mike Gillen
Gordon Harn
Col. Lindsey Henderson
Talley Kirkland
Ewell Lyle
Jack Magune
Richard Magune
Bill Marx
Patrick McDonald
Walter W. (Buck) Meeks III
Doris Phillip
Russell Phillips
Steve Price

Rusty "The Rock"
    Priestley
Jefferson C. Reed
Ralph Reed
Tommy Ridley
Ralph Righton
John Robeson
Gloria Smith-Ramsaur
Scott Smith
David Shuman
Edward Shuman
Henry Struble
Joe Thompson
John Thompson
Billy Townsend
Katie White
R. Martin Willett

Institutions

Georgia Department of Natural Resources
Georgia Historical Society
U.S. Army Military History Institute

National Archives
Library of Congress

ABBREVIATIONS USED

USAMHI: U.S. Army Military History Institute
LC: Library of Congress
NA: National Archives
GDNR: Georgia Department of Natural Resources
FMSHP: Fort McAllister State Historic Park
BL: *Battles and Leaders*

INTRODUCTION

Fort McAllister was only one of many large, earthen fortifications built around Savannah, Georgia, during the Civil War. The threat initially came from the sea, so efforts were made to defend navigable waterways and entrances. Many of these forts and batteries were never tested, and some were abandoned after they had been built; however, Fort McAllister attracted a lot of attention from the Union because of its location. Situated at the mouth of the Ogeechee River, the fort controlled access to the river and protected important railroad and highway bridges that crossed upstream, as well as the numerous planters living on the river. The railroad bridge was an important link to Georgia's southwest interior, and the highway bridge gave access to Savannah's "back door." Another attraction that came along in the summer of 1862 was the blockade runner *Nashville*, which sought protection behind the guns of the fort but was bottled up in the river by the vigilant gunboats of the U.S. Navy.

In April 1862, Fort Pulaski—at the mouth of the Savannah River—was captured by Federal forces. A massive brick fort, it was felt to be impregnable, but newly developed rifled cannon turned the masonry walls into rubble. With Pulaski's fall, the question on the minds of Southerners was, "If this modern fort could not stand against these new guns, how could the many sand forts and batteries be expected to stand?" Fort McAllister provided the answer.

Throughout late 1862, U.S. Navy gunboats attacked the fort on several occasions, without result. In early 1863, the navy brought to bear four new ironclad Monitors armed with the largest and heaviest ordnance available at the time. These ironclads were tested against Fort McAllister before being sent against Charleston. The last attack, on March 3, 1863, pitted three new Monitors and supporting gunboats against the fort for seven hours without success. Being made of sand, all the damage the fort sustained could simply be shoveled back into place—it was easier to shovel sand back into place than a pile of broken brick. At Fort McAllister, the South showed that the era of masonry forts was gone, and sand and earth would be the new method of defense against rifled cannon and heavy artillery. The only success the U.S. Navy saw at Fort McAllister was in the destruction of the blockade-runner *Nashville*, which allowed itself to be exposed to the Federal guns on the ironclad *Montauk*.

For a year and a half, this the fort was left unmolested, but in late 1864, a new threat appeared from the western interior of the state, as Gen. William T. Sherman's army marched through the state from Atlanta. When they arrived outside Savannah, they needed to open a water route to a fleet waiting to supply Sherman's forces. On December 13, 1864, he sent a division of infantry against Fort McAllister. In spite of all the efforts made by the 150-man garrison to withstand the attack, it was overwhelmed by a mass assault made by over 3,500 Union soldiers. With the fall of the fort, the Ogeechee River was opened, Sherman had his supply route, and Savannah was doomed, being evacuated by Confederate forces a week later.

The fort was abandoned and forgotten after the war ended. However, in 1927, Henry Ford purchased the property as part of land holdings he put together to establish a winter residence on coastal Georgia. He renovated the fort in 1935–1936; however, upon his death in 1947, the fort deteriorated again. In 1960, the State of Georgia acquired the property and renovated the site as part of its Civil War Centennial observance.

The historical events that occurred at Fort McAllister are beyond living memory, although numerous written narratives exist whose words allow us to paint a mental picture of these events. However, we are fortunate that photography was just coming of age when the Civil War began, and images of the fort as it appeared in 1864 still exist, providing us with a window to another time. This book explores those images, as we look back to see what those who lived that reality actually saw. These photos also provide us with the only known images of Sherman's soldiers in the field, at the end of his March to the Sea. They also provide us with a "baseline" by which to compare how the fort has aged over time.

Today, visitors can walk the fort where men once fought and died. They can marvel at the huge earthen walls, built by hand, and pay homage to all the Americans who served in that conflict.

One
THE BATTERY AT GENESIS POINT

The serenity of Fort McAllister today belies the fact that it was once an inferno of fire, iron, steel, and lead. The whole range of human emotion, drama, and trauma played out around and upon its walls as the spotlight of history was directed upon it. While those who lived that reality are gone, the fort remains today as a silent witness to that reality. (Roger S. Durham.)

Joseph L. McAllister owned the property at Genesis Point where Fort McAllister would be located. Whether the fort took its name from Joseph's father or himself, the fort's ties to the McAllisters is clear. The four-gun battery built at Genesis Point in 1861 was called the "Genesis Point Battery." When the war started, Mr. McAllister organized a company of cavalry that served around the fort until sent to Virginia in the spring of 1864. Joseph McAllister was killed at Trevilian's Station in June 1864. (Caroline Clay Swiggart.)

Strathy Hall, the home of Joseph L. McAllister and family, had been purchased in 1817 by Joseph's father, who turned it into a successful rice plantation. The subsequent acquisition of other tracts of land brought the Genesis Point property into the land holdings of the McAllisters, and the operation of the property eventually fell to Joseph. (Caroline Clay Swiggart.)

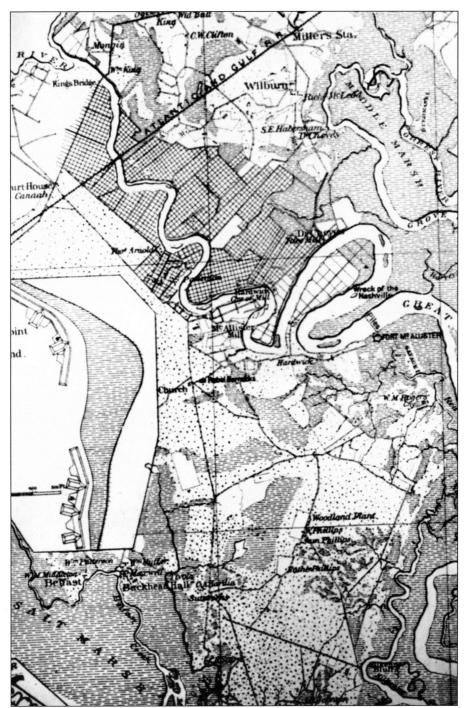

Genesis Point, at the mouth of the Ogeechee River, was the most logical point to control access to the river. A battery here protected the important railroad and highway bridges upstream. On the map, the coastal railroad from Savannah runs diagonally across the top at the upper right and the highway bridge is just upstream. Seven Mile Bend on the Ogeechee River is evident from the large loop the channel makes. (Roger S. Durham.)

Fort Beauregard, on Bay Point, Port Royal Sound, South Carolina, was typical of the defenses the Southerners built in the summer of 1861 on the offshore islands to protect access to inland waterways. Fort Beauregard, with Fort Walker across the sound to the south, protected Hilton Head Island and Port Royal Sound. The concept of massed cannons on an open parapet was thought to be more than adequate defense. (USAMHI.)

An 1861 view of a battery defending Pensacola, Florida, is shown here. In combat, the Southerners learned how open and vulnerable these gun mountings were. On November 7, 1861, a Federal fleet moved against Hilton Head, and the massed firepower of their warships made it impossible for the Southerners to serve these guns. The Confederates were forced to abandon the forts and offshore islands since they could not defend them without a navy to counteract the Northern navy. (USAMHI.)

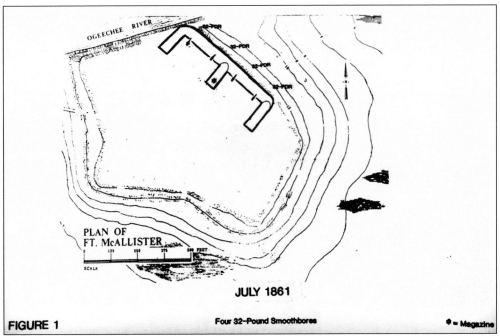

PLAN OF
FT. McALLISTER

JULY 1861

SCALE

FIGURE 1   Four 32-Pound Smoothbores   ♦ = Magazine

Company A, 1st Regiment Georgia Infantry, the Dekalb Rifles, arrived at Genesis Point on June 7, 1861, to construct a defense to protect the river's entrance. An analysis of information and evidence indicates that the first battery built there that summer consisted of two open bays separated by an earth-covered magazine, with two 32-pound smoothbore cannons in each bay. (Roger S. Durham.)

Construction of these defenses relied on local resources such as sand, mud, timber, lumber, and bricks, and slaves for a labor force. At Genesis Point, the defenses were carved out behind the low bluff, removing sand where it was not needed and placing it where fill was required. The earth was then packed down by teams of laborers armed with large wooden pestles to create a hard-packed earthen wall. (*Illustrated London*, April 18, 1863.)

13

A later view of the front wall of Fort McAllister is seen from outside the works. The large earthen "traverses" built between each gun provided lateral protection from flying shells and splinters. The men standing on the wall give a sense of scale as to the size and scope of the wall and the traverses. By providing the fort with this protection, an enemy would have to knock out each gun individually in order to destroy the fort. (LC.)

In July 1862, the Dekalb Rifles were ordered to Savannah and replaced by Company C, 1st Regiment Georgia Infantry, the Republican Blues, commanded by Capt. John Anderson, and Company F, 22nd Regiment Georgia Artillery, the Emmett Rifles, commanded by Capt. Augustus Bonaud. This image shows Pvt. Dougald Ferguson in the dress uniform of the Blues. He enlisted in 1857 and served at Fort McAllister. (Ferguson descendants Mr. Charles W. Seyle, Mrs. Lila Seyle Hooper, and Mrs. Gloria Smith-Ramsaur.)

This woodcut image of the Republican Blues in dress uniform is from the cover of *Frank Leslie's Illustrated* newspaper of August 4, 1860. The individuals depicted are, from left to right, Sgt. George W. Anderson Jr., 1st Lt. William H. Davis, Capt. John Anderson, 3d Lt. John T. McFarland, and 2d Lt. John Oliver.

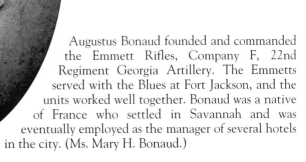

Augustus Bonaud founded and commanded the Emmett Rifles, Company F, 22nd Regiment Georgia Artillery. The Emmetts served with the Blues at Fort Jackson, and the units worked well together. Bonaud was a native of France who settled in Savannah and was eventually employed as the manager of several hotels in the city. (Ms. Mary H. Bonaud.)

These two views of a 32-pound smoothbore cannon at Fort McAllister illustrate the type of guns initially mounted in the battery. (LC.)

Two
IRON AND SAND

A 10-inch Columbiad in Fort McAllister stands guard over the river. The Columbiad was a large smooth-bore cannon. (NA.)

Fort Pulaski, on Cockspur Island, guarded the entrance to the Savannah River and represented the ultimate in coastal defense. Built of brick and stone, its thick walls were capable of withstanding anything that could be thrown against it. However, the advent of rifled artillery changed everything. On April 11, 1862, Federal forces brought a concentrated attack by rifled guns against the fort. Within 36 hours, the wall had been breached. (USAMHI.)

Federal rifled guns focused their fire on the southeast bastion of the fort and within hours had blasted a huge hole in the wall. Since Confederate defenders could not bring enough firepower to bear in response, they were at the mercy of the Federal guns. After 36 hours, the Confederate defenders raised the white flag and surrendered. (USAMHI.)

The fall of Fort Pulaski closed the Savannah River to Southern traffic. It also sounded the end of the era of brick and stone forts. For Southerners, the question was, "If this modern fort cannot withstand these new rifled cannon, how can the numerous sand forts scattered along the coast be expected to stand up?" Suddenly, they felt defenseless and at the mercy of the Federal navy. (USAMHI.)

Fort McAllister was attacked by a succession of wooden gunboats in July and November 1862 without success. On November 25, 1862, Maj. John B. Gallie assumed command of the post. He was a successful Savannah cotton merchant from Scotland who served with the Chatham Artillery for many years and organized several artillery units during the war. His death during the February 1, 1863 attack by the ironclad *Montauk* was the only casualty suffered by the garrison in seven major naval attacks. (GDNR.)

George W. Anderson Jr. served with the Republican Blues for many years and took command of the unit when his uncle, Capt. John Anderson, retired on November 11, 1862. George Anderson assumed command of the fort following the death of Major Gallie in February 1863, and command of the Blues fell to 1st Lt. William D. Dixon. Anderson would remain in command of the fort until its capture in December 1864. (GDNR.)

William D. Dixon joined the Republican Blues in March 1857 when he was 18. He rose through the ranks to command the unit by June 1863, when George Anderson assumed command of the fort. This photo of Capt. Dixon was taken in Savannah in June 1863. (Caroline T. Bosbyshell.)

James Madison Theus, a native of South Carolina, enlisted in the Republican Blues in April 1861 and served throughout the war with them. He eventually became the unit first sergeant and was elected second lieutenant in May 1863. He served on the 8-inch Columbiad gun commanded by William Dixon. After the war, Dixon married Theus's sister. (Caroline T. Bosbyshell.)

The U.S. Navy's Southeast Blockading Squadron was commanded by Samuel F. Dupont, seen at center. Operating out of Port Royal Sound, this squadron enforced the blockade of South Carolina, Georgia, and Florida, and supported operations against Charleston and Savannah. When U.S. Army operations against Charleston failed, the Navy Department wanted a naval victory and planned on using the new ironclad Monitors against the city. Dupont tested these new vessels against Fort McAllister before taking them against Charleston. (USAMHI.)

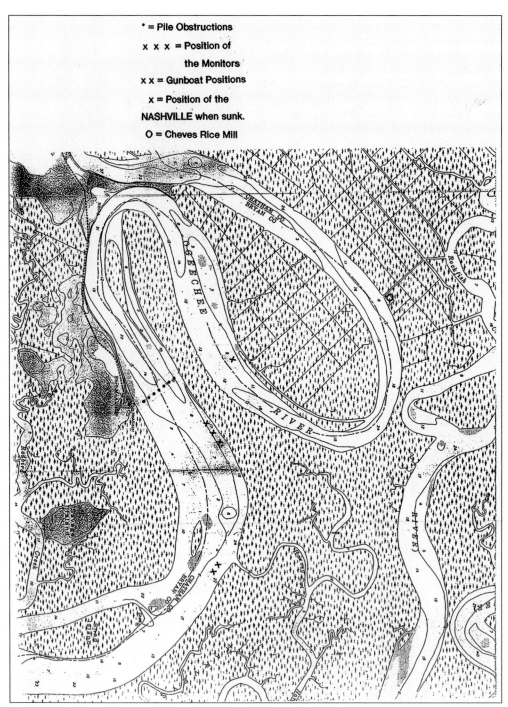

* = Pile Obstructions

x x x = Position of
      the Monitors

x x = Gunboat Positions

x = Position of the
NASHVILLE when sunk.

O = Cheves Rice Mill

This map shows Fort McAllister's location. (Roger S. Durham.)

John L. Worden, a native of New York, was sent to deliver secret orders to Union forces in Florida in 1861. He was captured by Southern forces and imprisoned for several months. Upon his return, he was assigned to command of the original *Monitor* and took that ironclad into battle against the Confederate ironclad *Virginia* in March of 1862. He then took command of the Monitor-class *Montauk* and supervised the ironclad attacks against Fort McAllister. (USAMHI.)

Percival Drayton commanded the ironclad *Passaic* during the March 3, 1863 attack on Fort McAllister. Drayton was a native of South Carolina, and his brother was an officer in the Confederate Army. At the attack on Hilton Head Island in November 1861, Drayton commanded one of the Federal warships, and his brother commanded Southern forces on Hilton Head. (NA.)

This is the 13-inch mortar aboard the schooner *Para*, part of the squadron that attacked Fort McAllister on March 3, 1863. The fort's low profile made it a hard target to hit. The use of mortar schooners allowed the navy to drop heavy shells into and around the fort. (USAMHI.)

The 13-inch mortar aboard the schooner *C.P. Williams* is seen here. The mortar schooners not only participated in the March 3, 1863 attack; they kept up a constant bombardment throughout the night in hopes that they could harass the garrison and prevent repairs from being made. (USAMHI.)

The 15-inch smoothbore Dahlgren gun fired a shell that weighed 330 pounds and required 50 pounds of powder. The armament of each Monitor included one 15-inch gun, and the men shown here give some idea of how large this gun was. Fort McAllister was the first place the 15-inch cannon was ever used in combat. Its shells completely penetrated the front wall of Fort McAllister, consisting of up to 18 feet of packed earth. (NA.)

This view of the fort shows where the Monitors took up position against the opposite bank of the river. The parapet here was penetrated several times. During the February 1, 1863 attack, a 15-inch shell came over the wall and struck a trunnion on the gun before exploding. Shrapnel from the explosion struck Major Gallie in the back of the head, killing him instantly. At that time, a 32-pound smoothbore gun was mounted here. The gun shown here is a 10-inch Columbiad emplaced in the summer of 1863. (LC.)

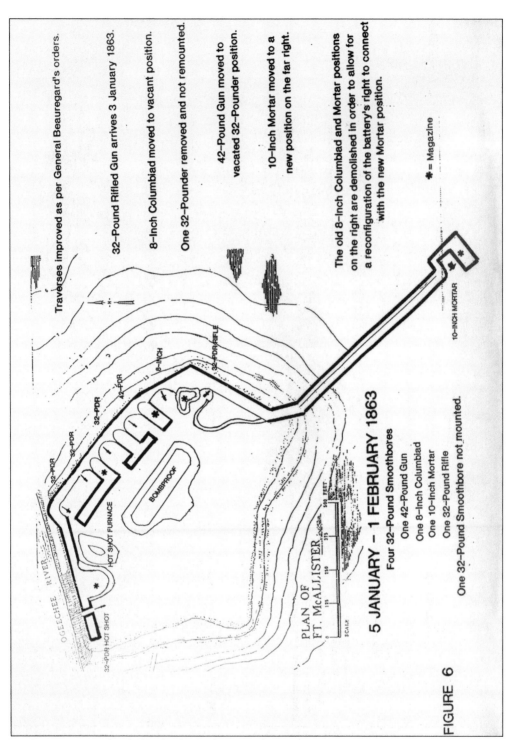

Within a year and a half, the little four-gun battery at Genesis Point had grown to be a formidable defense. Named Fort McAllister and mounting eight guns of heavy caliber, this is how the fort looked during the attacks of the U.S. ironclads. (Roger S. Durham.)

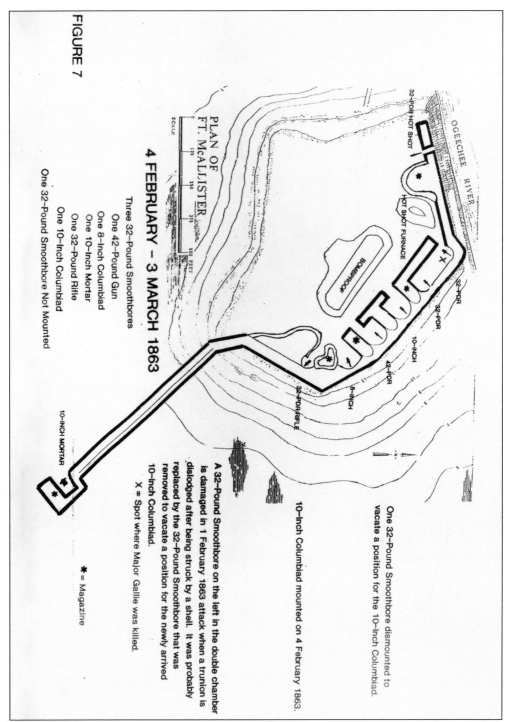

FIGURE 7

PLAN OF
FT. McALLISTER

SCALE

4 FEBRUARY – 3 MARCH 1863

Three 32-Pound Smoothbores
One 42-Pound Gun
One 8-Inch Columbiad
One 10-Inch Mortar
One 32-Pound Rifle
One 10-Inch Columbiad
One 32-Pound Smoothbore Not Mounted

OGEECHEE RIVER

32-PDR HOT SHOT

HOT SHOT FURNACE

BOMBPROOF

32-PDR

10-INCH

42-PDR

8-INCH

32-PDR RIFLE

10-INCH MORTAR

* = Magazine

One 32-Pound Smoothbore dismounted to
vacate a position for the 10-Inch Columbiad.

10-Inch Columbiad mounted on 4 February 1863.

A 32-Pound Smoothbore on the left in the double chamber
is damaged in 1 February 1863 attack when a trunion is
dislodged after being struck by a shell. It was probably
replaced by the 32-Pound Smoothbore that was
removed to vacate a position for the newly arrived
10-Inch Columbiad.

X = Spot where Major Gallie was killed.

After the initial attacks by the USS *Montauk*, it was withdrawn. Prior to the last naval assault on the fort, the task was taken up by the ironclads *Passaic*, *Nahant*, and *Patapsco* on March 3, 1863. This map shows changes made at Fort McAllister to prepare for this attack. (Roger S. Durham.)

27

This view from atop the bombproof looks across the front wall toward the position of the Monitors. The gun on the right is a 42-pound gun mounted in July 1862. During the March 3, 1863 attack, it was commanded by Lt. Daniel Quinn of the Emmett Rifles. The gun on the left is a 10-inch Columbiad, mounted on February 4, 1863. During the March 3, 1863 attack, it was commanded by Lt. William S. Rockwell of the Emmett Rifles. (LC.)

This 8-inch Columbiad was mounted following the July 29, 1862 attack. It was manufactured at the Tredegar Works in Richmond, Virginia, in 1861 and commanded by 1st Lt. William Dixon, who referred to it as his "pet gun." During the February 1, 1863 attack, the parapet was knocked down, exposing the gun, but the crew refused to abandon their position. During the March 3, 1863 attack, the gun carriage was shattered by a 15-inch shell, disabling the gun. There were no casualties among the gun crew. (LC.)

This was the only rifled piece of artillery in the fort. It was a "hybrid" gun, made by rifling a 32-pound smoothbore and applying a reinforcing band around the breech. It was brought to the fort on January 3, 1863, and during the February 1, 1863 attack, was commanded by Lt. Francis Willis of the Blues. During the March 3, 1863 attack, the gun crew was commanded by Cpl. Robert J. Smith of the Blues. (LC.)

This 10-inch seacoast mortar made at Tredegar Works in Richmond in 1862 had the serial number 1666. It was mounted on November 19, 1862; however, its firing caused damage to the walls and magazines, so it was moved out to a specially built emplacement. During the February 1 and March 3, 1863 attacks, the mortar was commanded by Capt. Robert Martin and a crew from his light battery, 3rd Company E 12th Battalion Georgia Light Artillery. (LC.)

This view of a 10-inch seacoast mortar at Pensacola, Florida, gives some idea of how the mortar at Fort McAllister would have looked when in use. During the March 3, 1863 attack, the mortar was able to drop shells on the flat decks of the Monitors. When it appeared that they were exploding harmlessly, Captain Martin had the powder removed from the shells and replaced with sand, making them heavier. In this way, he hoped to penetrate the deck armor. (NA.)

The ironclad *Montauk* is seen here after the war. (NA.)

The ironclad *Lehigh* shows something of what the Monitors would have looked like in the Ogeechee River at Fort McAllister. (NA.)

The accuracy of the gunners in Fort McAllister was well known, but their only hope of injuring the Monitors was to put a shot into one of the open gun ports of the turrets. The Monitors revolved their turrets so the back faced the fort while they reloaded, then turned back around to fire. This view of the *Patapsco* shows how closely they came to hitting their mark. The sailor on the left stands by the muzzle of the 15-inch Dahlgren. The other gun is a 200-pound Parrott Rifle. (USAMHI.)

The rear of the *Patapsco's* turret also took its share of punishment from the Confederate gunners. (USAMHI.)

With the Monitors' flat decks, the only targets for Confederate gunners were the turret, pilothouse, and smokestack. This image clearly shows the effects of Confederate shot on the smokestack of the *Passaic*. This view was taken at one of the repair shops at Hilton Head, where the damaged smokestack was being replaced. (USAMHI.)

Here is another view of the same smokestack. Captions with the original photos are confusing, since one is identified as being from the *Passaic*, while the other is identified as being from the *Patapsco*. A careful examination of the two photos shows that they are the same smokestack taken from different angles. (USAMHI.)

Two Monitors lie at anchor in a river at Hilton Head Island, South Carolina. The one at left is tied up to a lightship, while downstream the ironclad *Nahant* lies at anchor next to a tender. (USAMHI.)

The ironclad *Nahant* is tied up next to a tender at Hilton Head Island. The canopies over the deck and turret protect the crew from the hot sun. The flat iron deck quickly turned the interior of the ironclad into an oven with the sun beating down. (USAMHI.)

During the March 3, 1863 attack, sand-filled 10-inch shells from the mortar at Fort McAllister were dropped on the flat decks of the Monitors, causing damage to the thinly armored deck plates. Following this attack, Dupont ordered additional deck plating laid down over the most vulnerable parts of the vessel. This image clearly shows this new deck plating on the *Nahant*. (USAMHI.)

This view of naval officers aboard the *Patapsco* shows the new layer of deck plates as well as damage to the rear of the turret. (USAMHI.)

This is another view of naval officers aboard the *Patapsco*. On January 15, 1865, the *Patapsco* struck a torpedo near Charleston and quickly sank with almost its entire crew. (USAMHI.)

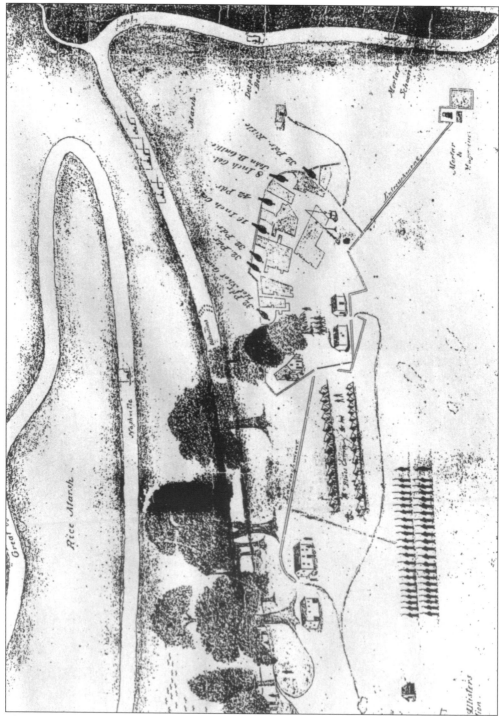

This sketch map of Fort McAllister was drawn by a member of the Republican Blues sometime following the March 3, 1863 attack on the fort by the ironclads *Passaic*, *Patapsco*, and *Nahant*. (Col. Lindsey Henderson.)

Three
THE NASHVILLE

Built in 1854 in New York City, the *Nashville* worked the East Coast and Trans-Atlantic routes. When the war began, it was seized by Southern authorities in Charleston and placed in government service. Armed with cannon, it was sent to England to obtain supplies in November 1861. Off the coast of Ireland it overtook and burned the clipper *Harvey Birch*, one of the first Confederate privateer captures, and flew the first Confederate flag seen in European waters. (GDNR-FMSHP.)

After making a series of successful runs through the blockade, the *Nashville* was sold to Fraser, Trenholm, & Company, who renamed it the *Thomas L. Wragg*. On July 23, 1862, it was thwarted in an attempt to run into Charleston and pursued down the coast to the Ogeechee River, where Fort McAllister protected it. Its cargo was unloaded at the railroad bridge and a new cargo was taken on, but the U.S. Navy blocked the entrance to the river, preventing its escape. (*Harper's Weekly*-FMSHP.)

Due to the vigilance of the U.S. Navy, the *Thomas L. Wragg* (*Nashville*) was unable to slip out. It was sold to Capt. T. Harrison Baker, who converted it into a privateer named the *Rattlesnake*. In the morning darkness of February 27, 1863, Baker ran it aground opposite the fort. Attempts to free the vessel failed, and on the morning of February 28, 1863, the *Montauk* struck the stranded privateer by firing across the marsh and destroyed it. (BL, v.4, p.29.)

While the gunners in the fort tried to distract the *Montauk* from its mission, the ironclad focused its attentions upon the stranded side-wheeler by firing across the marsh. (BL, v.4, p. 29.)

On its way downstream following the destruction of the *Rattlesnake*, the *Montauk* detonated a river torpedo beneath its hull, rupturing a number of hull plates. Threatened with the possibility of sinking, the pilot put the injured ironclad on a mud bank where the falling tide left it aground. This action stopped the water from entering the hull until temporary repairs could be made. By the time the rising tide floated the vessel, it was seaworthy enough to be taken to repair yards. (BL, v.4, p. 32.)

An aerial view of Seven Mile Bend, opposite Fort McAllister, shows the channel where the *Rattlesnake* (*Nashville*) was sunk. The area of the wreck is noted at center. This view is to the northeast, toward the city of Savannah. (GDNR.)

The Seven Mile Bend of the Ogeechee River is shown here. The *Rattlesnake* (*Nashville*) was sunk at center, as designated. The river loops back again and crosses the picture at lower right, passing in front of Fort McAllister. (GDNR.)

This view is opposite the previous picture, looking southwest toward the area of Hardwick. Old rice fields are evident at lower right. The area of the *Rattlesnake's* sinking is designated at center. Fort McAllister is located just out of picture to the left. (GDNR.)

This aerial view from over Fort McAllister's location looks across Seven Mile Bend. The *Rattlesnake's* location when sunk is designated at right center. (GDNR.)

This aerial view looks southeast toward Fort McAllister, designated by the arrow at upper right. The *Rattlesnake* (*Nashville*) lies at right center, shown by circle. Savage Island is seen at upper center and Ossabaw Sound in the upper distance. The old rice fields are evident in the foreground, where the straight lines through the marsh mark old canals and feeder trunks. (GDNR.)

In September 1960, the State of Georgia salvaged portions of the wreck in an attempt to remove navigational hazards. The salvage barge is seen here positioned over the wreck. (GDNR.)

This view shows remains of the vessel's driveshaft supports, still in place. These were exposed at low tide, but when the tide was high, they lurked just below the surface and could seriously damage unsuspecting vessels operating in the river. (GDNR.)

Divers prepare to remove a driveshaft support from the wreck in 1960. (GDNR.)

This photo and the following five views show the removal of a section of driveshaft supports from the wreck of the *Rattlesnake* (*Nashville*.) (GDNR.)

One section of the driveshaft support mechanism is brought up. (GDNR.)

Another section of the driveshaft support mechanism is lowered onto the deck of the salvage barge. (GDNR.)

Workers secure the section of driveshaft supports on deck of the salvage barge. (GDNR.)

The lifting hooks are removed from a section of driveshaft supports.

Recovered machinery parts from the wreck are seen on the deck of the salvage barge. (GDNR.)

One of the two operating levers that connected the engine to the driveshaft is being recovered from the wreck. The workman on the barge at far right gives an idea of the size of the piece. (GDNR.)

After recovery, the machinery parts were taken to Fort McAllister and off-loaded there to be displayed at the museum site. At that time, in 1960, the State of Georgia was in the process of renovating and developing a historic site at the fort. (GDNR.)

After the machinery parts were off-loaded, National Guard troops and equipment were used to move the heavy machinery parts from the water's edge up to the area where they would be displayed. (GDNR.)

The recovered machinery parts are being placed at Fort McAllister. (GDNR.)

Machinery parts at Fort McAllister await
final placement for display. (GDNR.)

A driveshaft support is still visible today at low tide. (Roger S. Durham.)

This photo of a dynamite detonation, used to break away machinery parts on the wreck during the 1960 salvage operation, brings to mind the water geysers seen in the river during naval attacks as shells plunged into the water around the Monitors and gunboats. (GDNR.)

Four

SHERMAN COMES

This detail from an 1864 photo of Fort McAllister shows saddles and horse equipment on racks inside the fort. It is evidence of the rarely considered numbers of horses kept in and around the fort. With two light batteries assigned to the garrison by late 1864, there would have been over 40 horses kept there. (NA.)

After fighting their way to the city of Atlanta in the spring and summer of 1864, Gen. William T. Sherman's forces captured the city in September. In November, Sherman cut his line of supply and communication to the North, and with 60,000 of his best men, he marched into the interior of Georgia. When they arrived outside Savannah, their supplies were low, and it became critically important to open a water route to a fleet of supply vessels waiting offshore. (USAMHI.)

Gen. Oliver O. Howard, a native of Maine, had served in the Eastern Theater of the war, losing an arm at the Battle of Fair Oaks in 1862. Sent to the Western Theater in early 1864, he served admirably under Sherman, commanding the right wing of his army during the March to the Sea. When the army reached the Georgia coast, Howard was responsible for opening a water route to the ocean. He sent scouts down the Ogeechee River in a small canoe to alert the navy to Sherman's presence then focused on capturing Fort McAllister, the last obstacle to opening the river. (USAMHI.)

Brig. Gen. Hugh Judson Kilpatrick, also a veteran of service in the Eastern Theater with the Army of the Potomac, was sent to the Western Theater in early 1864. He commanded Sherman's cavalry on the March to the Sea and fought Confederate Gen. Joseph Wheeler's forces virtually the entire way. When they reached the coast, he was initially tasked to capture Fort McAllister; however, General Howard had reservations about the ability of cavalry to take the fort, and in the end, it was decided to send infantry forces. (USAMHI.)

Brig. Gen. William B. Hazen, commander of the 2nd Division, 15th Army Corps, was ordered to move his division against Fort McAllister. This division was Sherman's old unit, which he had commanded early in the war at Shiloh and other battles. Sherman was confident in their ability to take the fort. The division of 5,000 men moved against Fort McAllister early on the morning of December 13, 1864. (USAMHI.)

Lt. Col William Strong, who served as Sherman's chief of staff during the March to the Sea, stood atop the Cheves rice mill with Sherman on December 13, 1864, and witnessed the assault on Fort McAllister from that vantage point. He also accompanied Sherman and Howard to the fort that evening, following its capture. (USAMHI.)

Capt. Francis DeGress commanded Battery H, 1st Illinois Artillery. His guns were the focal point of the fighting at the Hurt House during the Battle of Atlanta, and on December 12, 1864, his section of 20-pound Parrott rifles emplaced at the Cheves rice mill brought Fort McAllister under a harassing fire from across the marsh to the northwest. His guns would also fire the first artillery rounds into downtown Columbia, South Carolina, a few months later. (USAMHI.)

Gen. William J. Hardee commanded the Confederate forces defending Savannah. A former career U.S. Army officer, Hardee provided notable service to the Confederacy. At Savannah, he had about 10,000 men to man a defense that ringed the city. With Federal forces at Hilton Head, an active Union naval force offshore, and Sherman's army confronting him on the west, Hardee was in a difficult position. However, he held off Sherman for two weeks and was able to extricate his command from the trap that Savannah became. (USAMHI.)

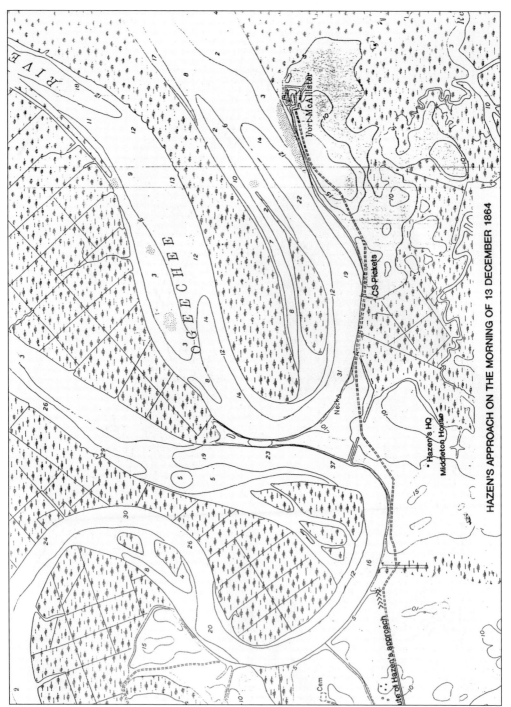

This map shows the approach of Hazen's Division to Genesis Point. (Roger S. Durham.)

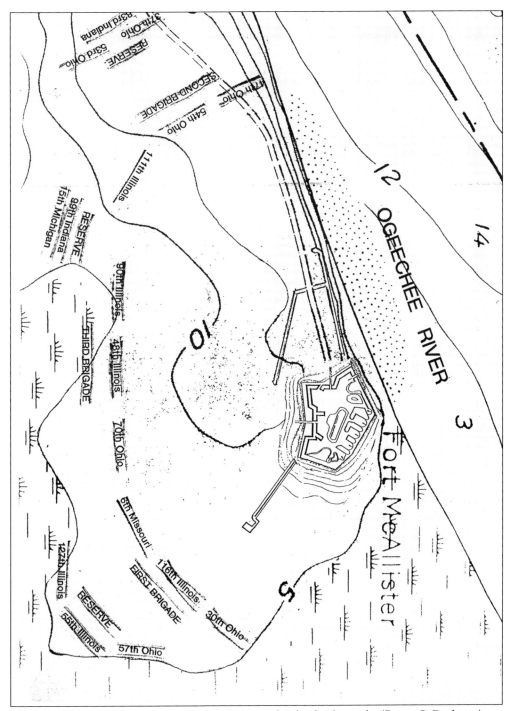

This map shows the deployment of Hazen's troops for the final assault. (Roger S. Durham.)

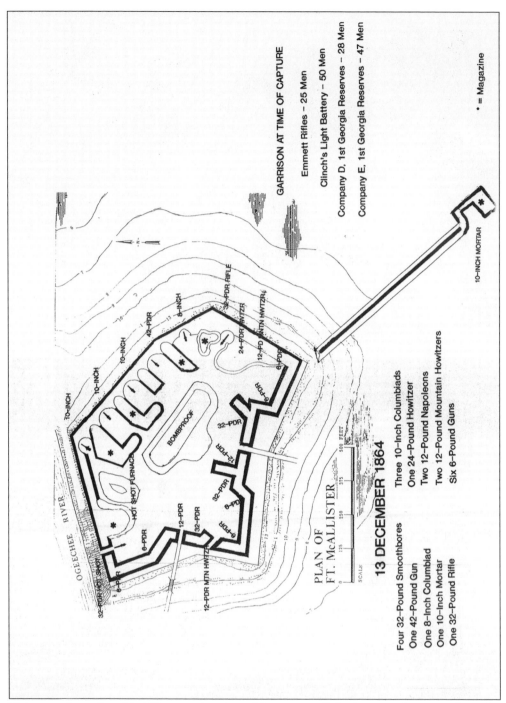

GARRISON AT TIME OF CAPTURE

Emmett Rifles – 25 Men

Clinch's Light Battery – 50 Men

Company D, 1st Georgia Reserves – 28 Men

Company E, 1st Georgia Reserves – 47 Men

• = Magazine

PLAN OF
FT. McALLISTER

13 DECEMBER 1864

Four 32–Pound Smoothbores   Three 10–Inch Columbiads

One 42–Pound Gun   One 24–Pound Howitzer

One 8–Inch Columbiad   Two 12–Pound Napoleons

One 10–Inch Mortar   Two 12–Pound Mountain Howitzers

One 32–Pound Rifle   Six 6–Pound Guns

This map shows Fort McAllister at the time of its capture. It had come a long way from the small, four-gun sand battery built in June 1861. (Roger S. Durham.)

Five

THE FINAL ASSAULT

A side-wheel steamer, moving either to or from the dock, has been captured as a blur in this detail image of a 1864 photo taken at Fort McAllister. This image illustrates what it was all about—communication with the outside world by water. (NA.)

This view from the 10-inch Columbiad position on the river looks upstream toward the rear approaches to the fort and shows the ground across which the 2nd Brigade approached (47th, 54th Ohio, and 111th Illinois Infantry.) The 47th Ohio approached below the river bluff at far right. Remnants of the Confederate obstructions that covered the rear approaches can be seen gathered in large piles for disposition. This view clearly shows something of what the Confederate defenders would have seen on December 13, 1864. (LC.)

Looking from the top of the bombproof across the west wall, this image shows the ground across which the 47th Ohio Infantry charged along the river bluff and gives an impression of what Confederate defenders would have seen. The river trench and an exterior rear trench visible here were part of an earlier rear defense system. (LC.)

Looking from the top of the bombproof out across the southwest bastion is the ground across which the 111th Illinois Infantry would have charged. An exterior trench, visible running diagonally from the right, was part of an earlier rear defense of the fort. The remains of obstructions are piled up for burning, but the last line of abatis is still in place and visible just under the brow of the wall. A 12-pound mountain howitzer remains in position to the right, covering the approach of a footbridge that entered the fort. This gun was the one that fired the shot in the incident described in the top image on page 69. (LC.)

This view looks out across the rear of the fort and shows the ground across which the Federal 3rd Brigade advanced (48th Illinois, 70th Ohio, and 15th Michigan Infantry.) (LC.)

This gun, firing en barbette—over the wall and not through an embrasure, or hole in the wall—shows how exposed Confederate gunners were to converging small-arms fire. Confederate infantrymen would have stood on the firing step behind the wall. (LC.)

The 32-pound cannon mounted at left is one of two that were moved to positions on the rear just before the arrival of Sherman's troops. The fresh dirt upon which the gun sits is clear evidence of its very recent construction. The camp behind the fort belongs to the 70th Ohio Infantry. (LC.)

A view of the fort shows how it would have appeared to the men of the Federal 1st Brigade (6th Missouri, 116th Illinois, and 30th Ohio Infantry) approaching from the right on the line of assault. The interior line of abatis obstruction is still in place, and the two soldiers standing on the wall at center give a sense of scope to this image. (LC.)

Col. Wells S. Jones of the 54th Ohio Infantry commanded the 2nd Brigade in the assault. About 3:30 p.m., Colonel Jones, accompanied by his adjutant Capt. John H. Groce, were scouting the ground across which his units would have to attack. Being in advance of the line, they attracted small-arms fire from the fort. One bullet passed through Captain Groce, killing him instantly, and struck Colonel Jones, seriously wounding him. He survived, and in the winter of 1947, his son Williard T.S. Jones visited the fort. (USAMHI.)

The fort is seen from the mortar magazine viewing to the northwest. This is how the fort would have appeared to the men of the 116th Illinois and 30th Ohio Infantry. The covered way between the fort and the mortar emplacement is seen at left. (LC.)

Another view of the fort shows how it would have appeared to the advancing Federal troops of the 111th Illinois Infantry. A line of buried torpedoes was located just in front and behind this line of abatis, so the open ground shown here would have held these devices. Ahead of the advancing troops lay the torpedoes and abatis shown here, another torpedo line, then the moat filled with palisades, and then the wall of the fort itself. (LC.)

The final assault is shown in a newspaper illustration of the period. Flags of the 47th Ohio Infantry (left) and the 70th Ohio Infantry (right) are shown on the wall. (*Harper's Weekly*, January 14, 1865.)

The waterfront behind the fort shows the bluff and marsh area across which the 47th Ohio Infantry advanced in order to bypass the Confederate abatis obstructions. Their attack was directed at the northwest bastion. (LC.)

The opposite view of the previous photo shows the fort as it appeared to the men of the advancing 47th Ohio Infantry. Their footprints in the marsh mud are still clearly evident in this photograph, showing the exposed beach after the tide had dropped. (LC.)

The river face of the fort is shown as it would have appeared to the men of the 47th Ohio Infantry. (LC.)

The northwest bastion is seen under attack by the men of the 47th Ohio Infantry. (*Harper's Weekly*, January 14, 1865.)

The northwest bastion, where heavy fighting ensued for the men of the 47th Ohio Infantry, is shown here. A 6-pound field gun was positioned on this platform. Initially, the Confederate defenders were surprised by the attack coming out of the marsh, but they were able to hold the attackers back until overwhelmed by sheer force of numbers. (LC.)

The western glacis outside the fort shows the head of the footbridge and the area the 54th Ohio Infantry crossed. Lt. Col. William Strong wrote, "a daring color sergeant drives down his flagstaff upon the escarpment while the color guard group about him to protect the flag; the next instant all are cut down and swept away at one discharge from a light howitzer and the colors lie in the ditch torn to shreds and covered with blood and mangled corpses of its brave defenders." The howitzer Strong speaks of was located just out of picture to the right and is visible in the top image on page 61. (LC.)

The assault on the rear of the fort by the men of the 48th Illinois, 70th Ohio, and 15th Michigan Infantry is shown as they make their way through the obstructions and palisades in the moat. (*Harper's Weekly*, January 14, 1865.)

The rear wall of the fort is shown as it was seen by the men of the 3rd Brigade (48th Illinois, 70th Ohio, and 15th Michigan Infantry), showing the glacis at right, the moat, and row of palisades they had to pass. (LC.)

Pvt. Charles Degman of the 70th Ohio wrote that they "came to the ditch in the bottom of which were planted firmly a line of sharp-pointed stakes four or five feet high, set at an angle . . . pointing outward. This was a serious obstacle, as the stakes could not be moved except in a few cases. Some got thru the small openings, some were held up by comrades, and fell over, others were helped over by those on the other side. Finally all were over, and then came the command from Col. Phillips: 'Forward, boys!' They fired one volley and then, with bayonet in hand, leaped forward and in only a few minutes . . . were on top of the fort." (LC.)

This is the opposite view of the top image on page 67, looking back across the rear of the fort and showing the ground across which the 3rd Brigade advanced. The exterior glacis is clearly evident to the left of the picture where the wheelbarrows sit. (LC.)

Lt. Colonel Strong wrote, "Our troops fairly swarmed about the fort and on the parapet, a dozen flags could be seen and though here and there one would disappear from sight—yet there were plenty of brave fellows to hold it up again." Maj. George W. Nichols wrote, "Crowds of men were visible on the parapets. . . . Then the bomb-proofs and parapets were alive with crowding swarms of our gallant men." (*Harper's Weekly*, January 14, 1865.)

Now, the fighting moved to the interior of the fort. These views show the parade ground of the fort, where fighting continued to rage as Federal attackers swarmed over the wall. Major Anderson was knocked down by a Federal soldier wielding a clubbed musket, before Brigadier General Hazen took custody of him. Hazen and Anderson had known one another before the war. Many Confederates continued the fight from the bombproof and magazines until they were all eventually overcome. (LC.)

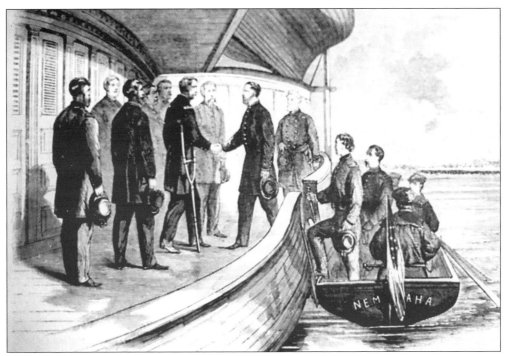

That evening General Sherman and General Howard were taken downstream to meet with Gen. John Foster aboard the revenue cutter *Nemaha*. Once the Ogeechee River was cleared of obstructions and torpedoes, critically needed supplies could be shipped in to support Sherman's forces. (*Harper's Weekly*, January 14, 1865.)

Lt. William Sherfy of the Army Signal Corps established a signal station on the front wall of the occupied fort as a means of communicating with shipping in the river, as well as with other elements of Sherman's army across the marsh. (LC.)

The 70th Ohio was given the honor of garrisoning the fort and was tasked with the mission of removing the ammunition and dismantling the artillery. They were assisted by work details from the 55th Illinois who were camped at nearby Whitehall Plantation. This image shows the camp of the 70th Ohio behind the fort, on the same ground they charged across only days before. (LC.)

A group assembles at the dismounting of a 10-inch Columbiad. They wear an assortment of overcoats and headgear. (LC.)

Here is another view of the group seen in the previous photo. (LC.)

A group of five soldiers takes a break on the shade. (LC.)

A working party removes 10-inch explosive ball ammunition. The wear and tear is clearly evident on the jackets of these men. Also, the inside pocket over the left breast can be seen on each jacket as they are filled with each man's personal items. The fit of army clothes is also illustrated here. Headwear is the Hardee hat, well worn and altered to meet the approval of the wearer. (LC.)

A dismantled gun carriage and truck are seen at the bottom of the bombproof near the sally port. (LC.)

Soldiers lounge about the fort, aware of the history they had just written, but unaware of the events that had occurred a year and a half earlier between the U.S. Navy and the Confederate defenders. (LC.)

Stacked arms of Federal soldiers are seen at Fort McAllister. The wheelbarrow indicates that they have work of a different nature before them. (NA.)

The guns of Fort McAllister are silenced forever. (LC.)

Six

THE 20TH CENTURY

These laborers working for Mr. Henry Ford during his renovation of Fort McAllister evoke memories of their ancestors who also toiled there 75 years earlier under much different circumstances. (FMSHP.)

From left to right, Mr. Will Donaldson, Mr. Henry Ford, and Mr. George Gregory (superintendent of Richmond Hill Plantation) dig out the hot shot furnace. This photo was taken in the spring of 1935. (FMSHP.)

Mr. Will Donaldson digs into the hot shot furnace in the spring of 1935. (FMSHP.)

Mr. Will Donaldson, at left, and Mr. George Gregory dig out the original hot shot furnace. (FMSHP.)

Workmen uncover the brickwork of the original hot shot furnace. (FMSHP.)

The hot shot furnace is exposed after excavation is complete. (FMSHP.)

Mr. Bob Bryan and Mr. Charles Sorenson are pictured in an excavated portion of the fort in 1935. (FMSHP.)

Mr. George Gregory, standing at left, discusses renovation work being done near the bombproof. (FMSHP.)

The bombproof is seen after it was taken down. To the right, Mr. Henry Ford and Mr. Charles Sorenson walk on the exposed timbers of the original bombproof's floor in 1935. (FMSHP.)

Exposed timbers from the collapsed bombproof are seen during the reconstruction work in 1935. (FMSHP.)

Shown here is the bombproof during renovation work taking place under Mr. Ford's supervision. (FMSHP.)

A view of the fort and hot shot furnace is seen here following Ford's renovation of the fort. Mr. Ford's road into the fort is seen to the left, where the hot shot gun (Number 1 gun position) had been placed. For some reason, Ford removed this portion of the wall and placed a road through here to access the interior of the fort. (GDNR.)

Mr. Ford mounted this 18th-century iron cannon tube in the Number 2 gun position on the river angle. The gun carriage was made of live oak in the workshops of the Ford Technical School at Richmond Hill. (GDNR.)

This is the same view taken 40 years later. The cannon fell victim to vandals and scrap drives, but the carriage remained until the mid-1980s, when it was recognized as an artifact in its own right and removed. (Roger S. Durham.)

After Ford's death in 1947, his property in Bryan County was sold off. Fort McAllister was owned by a local paper company until 1960, when the State of Georgia acquired the property in order to develop a historic site as part of Georgia's Civil War Centennial celebration. Since the fort had not been maintained, much of Ford's renovation work had deteriorated. These two views show the hot shot furnace at the time the State took possession of the property. (GDNR.)

The entrance to the bombproof shows Ford's masonry work, which was not representative of the original entry. (GDNR.)

When Ford had the magazines rebuilt, he used heavy timbers, just as they had originally been built. Over the years, however, the timbers rotted and the magazines collapsed. This view shows the entrance to one magazine and the condition of the timbers as they appeared in 1958. (GDNR.)

A partially intact magazine entrance and tunnel illustrate the condition of Mr. Ford's renovation in 1958. (GDNR.)

The collapsed entrance to one of the Ford renovated magazines is seen here. (GDNR.)

Mr. Ford's cannon carriage in the Number 2 gun position is seen in 1958. (GDNR.)

The same view is seen here 25 years later. (Roger S. Durham.)

Workmen begin construction of the museum building in 1960. (GDNR.)

The completed museum building is seen from the fort. (GDNR.)

The same view is pictured 25 years later. (Roger S. Durham.)

Restoration work on one of the magazines progresses in 1963. (GDNR.)

The magazine shown in the previous view is seen after its restoration was completed. (GDNR.)

The restored bombproof is shown here from the cut in the wall where the footbridge will be rebuilt. (GDNR.)

The interior parade ground of the restored fort is seen in 1963. During this time, the State attempted to restore the Number 1 gun position where the hot shot gun would have been located. (GDNR.)

The same view is pictured here 25 years later. (Roger S. Durham.)

The restored Number 2 gun position is seen in 1963. (GDNR.)

The same view is shown here 25 years later. (Roger S. Durham.)

The current Museum and Visitor's Center at Fort McAllister State Historic Park is pictured here. (Roger S. Durham.)

The grassy slopes and moss-covered trees provide a haunting atmosphere to the ground where men once fought and died in their struggle to control this small piece of real estate. (Roger S. Durham.)

Seven

FORT MCALLISTER
Then and Now

Samuel A. Cooley poses with his photographic wagon and the camera he probably took to Fort McAllister to make the following images. He arrived at the fort when it was being dismantled, and given the fact that most of the heavy guns were still in the fort, it is probable that the work had just begun. This places the time frame of these photos in the last two weeks of December 1864. In all probability, Savannah was still in Confederate hands when these photos were taken. (USAMHI.)

Mr. Samuel A. Cooley operated a photographic gallery in Beaufort, South Carolina. With the Federal occupation of Beaufort and Hilton Head, Cooley found employment taking "official" photos and made a prosperous business among the large number of soldiers and sailors who wanted photos taken for friends and families. He was well acquainted with Fort McAllister's reputation, and when it was captured, he availed himself of the chance to photograph the fort. (USAMHI.)

Cooley set up a portable darkroom in the southeast bastion of the fort. A funnel and bottles of chemicals sits on the fallen sentry box. Here, Cooley mixed the solutions and coated the glass plates used to make these photographic images of Fort McAllister. There is speculation that George Barnard took these images since he used a similar darkroom, but no images taken by him during the March to the Sea have been found, and Barnard's Savannah images were taken in February or March 1865. (LC.)

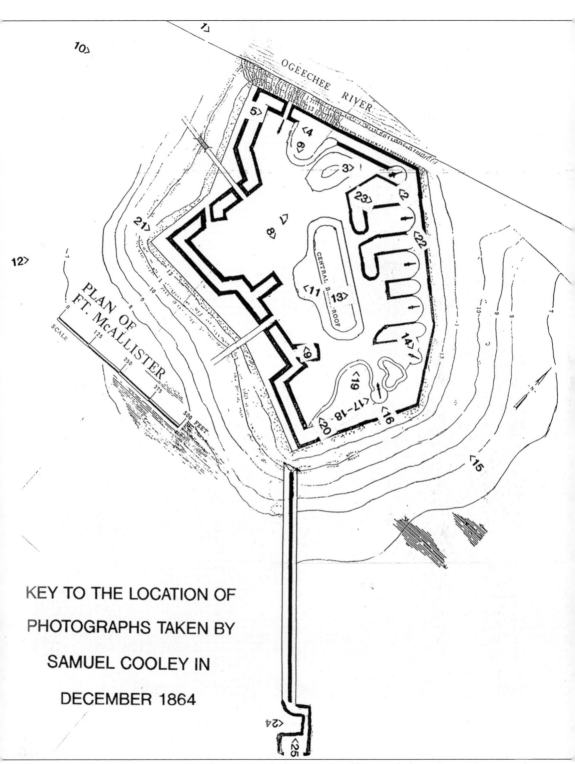

KEY TO THE LOCATION OF
PHOTOGRAPHS TAKEN BY
SAMUEL COOLEY IN
DECEMBER 1864

This map of the fort shows the locations of photographs illustrated throughout the rest of the book.

The river face of the fort, viewing downstream at low tide, is seen in these photographs, taken at point 1 on the map. The flagpole is seen at upper right center. The signal station on the wall is marked by a wedge tent seen at upper center. One man can be seen reclining in a chair in front of the tent, a signal flag stuck into the wall. A fire smolders on the shore. The marsh mud beach in the foreground still shows the footprints left by the men of the 47th Ohio Infantry as they approached the fort during the final assault. The picture below is the same view as seen today. (Above, LC; below, Roger S. Durham.)

Point 2 looks in the opposite direction from point 1, viewing along the river front. Smoke from the burning of Confederate abatis can be seen to the left rear. The fort's dock extends out into the river, and soldiers lounge on the dock awaiting the arrival of a steamer. At distant center, a guard stands with his back to the viewer and his foot propped on a wooden box. The pictures from point 4 will be taken from where he stands and will show us what he sees. The pictures from point 5 will be taken from a point behind the mound at left. The picture below shows the same view as seen today. (Above, LC; below, Roger S. Durham.)

Viewing in the opposite direction from point 2 is point 3, which shows the signal station and the river beyond. The steamer will soon come up to the fort's dock, since the pilings have been removed from the river. On December 12, 1864, when Captain DeGress's artillery brought the fort under fire from across the river, several of the fort's magazines were exposed to this fire. Captain Anderson had traverses built to protect these threatened magazines. One of these new traverses is seen at lower right, a wall of planking against which fresh earth has been piled. The same view as seen today is pictured below. (Above, LC; below, Roger S. Durham.)

Point 4 views upstream across the northwest bastion. The steamer in the previous view from point 3 is pulling up to the dock, and the soldiers are gathered at the end of the dock awaiting its arrival. On the vacant gun platform at center, a Federal soldier leans on a broom, where a short time before the men of the 47th Ohio struggled to take the bastion as they swarmed up out of the marsh to plant their flag on the parapet. In the foreground, the Number 1 gun (the hot shot gun) sits in its emplacement. The view from point 5 was taken from the wall near where the soldier stands. The camera was taken off the tripod, placed on the sandbags, and aimed back toward the viewer. Below is the same view as seen today. (Above, LC; below, Roger S. Durham.)

103

Point 5 is viewing back in the opposite direction from point 4, which was taken from atop the mound near the base of the flagpole. On the wall at upper left is the wooden box that the soldier in the photo at point 2 had propped his foot against. The image from point 6 will be taken from a point on the wall just out of frame to the right. The same view is pictured below as seen today. (Above, LC; below, Roger S. Durham.)

Point 6 looks southeast across the rear wall of the fort. The camp of the 70th Ohio Infantry is located to the rear, on the ground they had charged across days before. The fresh dirt of the gun emplacement at center indicates it had just been built to accommodate the 32-pound gun placed there. Blankets have been hung out on the gun carriage to dry. In the parade ground can be seen two stands of weapons and a wheelbarrow. Below is the same view as seen today. (Above, LC; below, Roger S. Durham.)

A working party removes 10-inch shells from the magazine of the Number 3 gun, located behind the mound with the flagpole on it, in this picture taken at point 7. The entrance to the hot shot furnace is seen at left, between and behind the first two soldiers at left. At the upper right the flagpole base can be seen. The photo at point 2 was taken from atop this traverse, and the photo at point 20 was taken from near the flagpole, looking into the 10-inch Columbiad position of the Number 3 gun on the opposite side. The same view as seen today is pictured below. (Above, LC; below, Roger S. Durham.)

The image from point 8 is just 90-degrees to the right of the previous image, at point 7. The bombproof is to the left, and at right, the traverse and gun position visible in the photograph from point 6 can be seen. The photo from point 9 was taken from the top of the traverse seen at distant center. Point 11's picture was taken from the top of the bombproof at left center. Note the large puddle of water present between the bombproof and the traverse. A gun carriage and truck from a dismantled Columbiad is seen piled beside the bombproof. The same view is pictured below as seen today. (Above, LC; below, Roger S. Durham.)

Viewing in the opposite direction from the previous photo, as seen from atop the traverse, is this picture from point 9. The bombproof is to the right, where a carriage and truck from a dismantled Columbiad have been placed. The gun platform at left is another of those constructed just before the arrival of Sherman's forces. In the center, where the large puddle of water is present in the picture at point 8, a group of soldiers can be seen leaning against the traverse and there is no water. This is evidence that the weather changed while Cooley was there. The northwest bastion is seen at distant upper right. The steamer seen in the pictures from points 3 and 4 is seen here joined by another steamer. The photo at point 11 was taken from atop the bombproof at right. The same view as seen today is pictured below. (Above, LC; below, Roger S. Durham.)

Point 10 looks northeast from outside the abatis line, looking back toward the head of the footbridge. This view was taken in the late afternoon as evidenced by the long shadows. The working party at center stands around the dismantled gun gin, seen in use in the pictures from points 21 and 22. A gun sling cart, possibly the one seen in the image from point 20, is visible at the left behind the wall of the northwest bastion. The bombproof is seen at center behind the work party. The flagpole is seen to the left. Below is the same view as seen today. (Above, LC; below, Roger S. Durham.)

The photo from point 11 looks southwest from the top of the bombproof out over the southwest bastion. The group of soldiers seen reclining at the lower center is the same as those seen in the photo from point 9. The footbridge entrance is to the far right. A barbette carriage minus the cannon tube sits in position on the parapet next to the footbridge entrance. The image from point 12 was taken from atop the trench seen in upper left background. The same view as seen today is pictured below. (Above, LC; below, Roger S. Durham.)

This picture is from point 12, viewing back in the opposite direction as the previous photo. The southwest bastion is at center, the bombproof directly behind that. The last line of abatis obstruction is in the foreground. The camera here was situated atop an exterior trench. The same view is pictured below as seen today. (Above, LC; below, Roger S. Durham.)

This image looks northeast from point 13 atop the bombproof out across the front of the fort toward the river beyond. A 10-inch Columbiad is seen at left in the Number 4 gun position, and to the right, the 42-pound gun is in the Number 5 gun position. Gun carriage and truck parts lay at the base of the traverse at center, and a broken wheelbarrow lays at lower right. Shadows indicate this view was taken in the late afternoon. Below is the same view as seen today. (Above, LC; below, Roger S. Durham.)

The number 6 on the cascabel in this picture taken from point 14 indicates that this is the 8-inch Columbiad in the Number 6 gun position commanded by William D. Dixon. This was Dixon's "pet gun." It gave a good accounting for itself during the naval attacks and was dismounted during the March 3, 1863 attack. Below is the same view as seen today. (Above, LC; below, Roger S. Durham.)

This view of the front face of the fort looking southwest was taken from point 15. The original battery wall is seen at right. To the far left is the 32-pound rifled gun in the Number 7 gun position, seen in photos from points 16, 17, and 18. The men standing on the wall are in front of the Number 6 gun position, where the 8-inch Columbiad—Dixon's "pet gun"—was located. The line of abatis is evident here, and the problem of erosion can be seen on the wall of the fort. The crater at left foreground gives evidence of the numerous naval bombardments. A road runs diagonally across the foreground. The same view as seen today is pictured below. (Above, LC; below, Roger S. Durham.)

The 32-pound rifled gun in the Number 7 gun position is pictured here looking west from point 16 in the morning sun. The bombproof is seen at upper center behind the gun. The photos from points 11 and 13 were taken from atop the bombproof. The image from point 9 was taken from atop the traverse to the far left. Pictured below is the same view as seen today. (Above, LC; below, Roger S. Durham.)

This is another view of the 32-pound rifled gun taken from point 17. The four soldiers in the background are probably the same four visible in the background of the picture from point 13. (LC.)

This view of the 32-pound rifled gun was taken after the previous photo, as evidenced by the movement of the sun on the breech of the cannon. The person at center could be either military or civilian. It is possible that it is the photographer, Cooley. (LC.)

This photo shows the view in the opposite two photos as seen today. (Roger S. Durham.)

The photographer turned the camera to the left and took an image across the back of the 32-pound rifled gun position and the bombproof beyond in this picture from point 19. The same view as seen today is shown below. (Above, LC; below, Roger S. Durham.)

The photographer turned the camera to the left again and took this image viewing west across the rear of the fort from point 20 on the southeast bastion toward the southwest bastion. In the lower foreground is an up-ended sentry box, and Cooley's portable darkroom sits beside it. An empty gun platform sits above the darkroom. Below is the same view as seen today. (Above, LC; below, Roger S. Durham.)

This image views southeast from point 21 across the rear wall in the opposite direction toward where the previous image was taken. In the foreground, the palisades in the moat are seen. Their stout construction is evident in the fact that so many are still in place in this photograph, taken after the assault and at least a week of occupation. A section has been removed at the angle in the lower center and a path is evident on the wall showing where soldiers from the camp have used this as an entry point. The traverse visible at upper left center was the vantage point for the image at point 9. The same view as seen today is pictured below. (Above, LC; below, Roger S. Durham.)

This image from point 22 shows soldiers dismounting the 10-inch Columbiad at the Number 3 gun position. The flagpole is seen atop the traverse at upper right. The 10-inch ammunition being taken out by wheelbarrow in the image from point 7 was being removed from the magazine for this gun. The direction of the sunlight indicates the time to be about 10:30 a.m. The image from point 2 was taken from atop the traverse to the right, and the image from point 23 was taken from atop the traverse from center background. The same view is pictured below as seen today. (Above, LC; below, Roger S. Durham.)

Point 23 shows the opposite view from the previous photo taken from atop the traverse showing the 10-inch Columbia being dismounted. The same view as seen today is pictured below. (Left, LC; below, Roger S. Durham.)

The 10-inch seacoast mortar in its emplacement can be seen in this image from point 24. Evidence of recent rains can be seen that indicate this photo was taken at the same time as the image from point 8. Below is the same view as seen today. (Right, LC; below, Roger S. Durham.)

The picture taken from point 25 views northwest from atop the mortar magazine looking back down the earthen wall of the "covered way" toward the fort in the background. The same view as seen today is pictured below. (Above, LC; below, Roger S. Durham.)

This picture shows the Confederate signal tower on the riverbank behind the fort. A chain of signal stations connected the fort to the bridge upstream and to Coffee Bluff, where telegraphs connected the fort to Savannah. Apparently the tower played no role in Sherman's assault, but the large tree trunks on the ground indicate that it was close enough to the assault that Confederate abatis had been put down. There are no features to identify where this tower stood. (NA.)

This view shows the original road to Fort McAllister running along the bluff through the state park. The large live oak at left witnessed the events that took place around it in 1861–1865. Today, picnic tables and playground equipment occupy the ground where men once fought and died. The panorama of serenity stands in contrast to the reality that once played out here. The fort stands as a monument to all Americans who served in that conflict. (Roger S. Durham.)

The grave of John Wayne Anderson is pictured here in Laurel Grove Cemetery in Savannah, Georgia. He commanded the Republican Blues for over 30 years and took them to Fort McAllister in August 1862. He resigned in November 1862. Command of the Republican Blues went to his nephew George W. Anderson Jr. (Roger S. Durham.)

The grave of George Nicoll in Laurel Grove Cemetery is pictured here. He was a member of the Republican Blues, and he was elected to command the Emmett Rifles when they reorganized in November 1862. (Roger S. Durham.)

Shown here is the grave of George W. Anderson Jr. in Laurel Grove Cemetery. He assumed command of the Republican Blues when his uncle resigned, and he was promoted to major when John B. Gallie was killed at the fort. Command of the Blues fell to William D. Dixon. George Anderson remained in command of Fort McAllister until its fall to Sherman in December 1864. (Roger S. Durham.)

This is the grave of John B. Gallie in Laurel Grove Cemetery. He was the only fatality suffered in all of the naval attacks. George W. Anderson assumed command of the fort following Gallie's death. Today, Anderson's grave lies very close to Gallie's. (Roger S. Durham.)

INDEX

15-inch Dahlgren, 25, 31
Anderson, George W. Jr., 15, 20, 72, 102
Anderson, John W., 14, 15
Baker, T. Harrison, 38
Bonaud, Augustus, 14, 15
Bryan, Robert, 84
Cheves Rice Mill, 54
Cooley, Samuel A., 97, 98, 108, 116, 119
USS *C.P. Williams*, 24
Davis, William H., 15
Degman, Charles, 70
Degress, Francis, 54, 102
Dekalb Rifles, 13, 14
Dixon, William D., 20, 21, 113
Donaldson, Will, 80, 81
Drayton, Percival, 23
DuPont, Samuel F., 21, 34
Emmett Rifles, 14, 15, 28
Ferguson, Dougald, 14
Ford, Henry, 79, 80, 83
Fort Beauregard, 12
Fort Jackson, 15
Fort Pulaski, 18, 19
Fort Walker, 12
Foster, John, 73
Gallie, John B., 18, 19
Genesis Point, 10, 13
Gregory, George, 80–82
Groce, John H., 63
Hardee, William J., 55
CSS *Harvey Birch*, 37
Hazen, William B., 53, 56, 57, 72
Hilton Head Island, South Carolina, 12, 23, 32–34, 55

Howard, Oliver O., 52–54, 73
Jones, Wells S., 63
Kilpatrick, Hugh J., 53
USS *Lehigh*, 31
Martin, Robert, 29, 30
McAllister, Joseph L., 10
McFarland, John T., 15
USS *Montauk*, 19, 23, 28, 30, 38, 39
USS *Nahant*, 33–35
CSS *Nashville*, 37, 38, 40–42, 44
USS *Nehama*, 73
Nichols, George W., 71
Oliver, John, 15
USS *Para*, 24
USS *Passaic*, 23, 32, 33
USS *Patapsco*, 31–33, 35
Pet gun, 21, 28, 113, 114
Quinn, Daniel, 28
CSS *Rattlesnake*, 38–42, 44
Republican Blues, 14, 15, 20, 21, 29
Rockwell, William S., 28
Sherfy, William, 73
Sherman, William T., 52–54, 73
Smith, Robert J., 29
Sorenson, Charles, 83, 84
Strathy Hall, 10
Strong, William, 54, 69, 71
Theus, James M., 21
CSS *Thomas L. Wragg*, 38
Wheeler, Joseph, 53
Willis, Francis, 29
Worden, John L., 23